ALSO BY JOAN WICKERSHAM

The News from Spain

The Suicide Index

The Paper Anniversary

JOAN WICKERSHAM

———

NO SHIP
SETS OUT
TO BE
A SHIPWRECK

———

EASTOVER
■ PRESS ■

ISBN: 978-1-958094-53-2

EastOver Press encourages the use of our publications
in educational settings. For questions about educational discounts,
contactus online: www.EastOverPress.com or info@EastOverPress.com.

1 2 3 4 5 6 7 8 9 10

Published in the United States of America by

EASTOVER PRESS
Rochester, Massachusetts
www.EastOverPress.com

For Tom and Alec

"I wanted unlucky ships, those that were lost with crew and all."
—ANDERS FRANZÉN

———————

"Our possessions will outlast us, we'll desert them in the end."
—IAN MCEWAN

CONTENTS

III. THE DRY DOCK

IV. FURTHERMORE

V. SHIPWORM

NO SHIP
SETS OUT
TO BE
A SHIPWRECK

On August 10, 1628, only minutes into her maiden voyage, the Swedish warship Vasa sank in Stockholm harbor, capsized by a small gust of wind that came down through a gap in the cliffs.

For more than three hundred years the Vasa lay, largely forgotten, in the mud at the bottom of the harbor, until 1956 when Anders Franzén, an independent researcher, rediscovered the wreck using a grappling hook and a homemade core sampling tool.

The Vasa was raised and restored, and a museum was built to house the ship and everything found with her, including the bones of the people who had died in the wreck.

BEFORE WE BEGIN

I wasn't really interested in going to the museum. But my husband had read about the ship in *National Geographic* as a child and he'd never forgotten the story. "Great," I said, trying to be a good sport. My husband had always liked maritime history. The week before, in Denmark, we had seen some Viking ships, open boats with scrolled prows; I thought the *Vasa* would probably be something like that.

This was our first visit to Stockholm. A city of hills, blasted out of the rocky islands. A city of metal and glass and right angles, but also made up of street after curving street of *fin de siècle* apartment houses, stone or brick or gently colored stucco – creams and yellows and ochres – swelling with bays and dormers, turrets and Baltic onion domes. Staid, elephantine, yet playful too, as if someone had inflated them with air; they rollicked up and down the sloping streets. My husband and I would come, suddenly, to a staircase or tunnel, and we'd see a whole further layer of these voluptuous buildings spreading far above or below. Or we would look between the buildings and see boats and sparkling water; and the street we were walking on would turn into a bridge.

A dream city: the place you come to that seems familiar even though you've never been there before. You know which way to turn at the corner, you love the light and recognize the sky. You're fatuous, a tourist. You skim along the surface, looking at paintings, browsing in shops, eating food someone else has cooked. You see parents hurrying through the streets with their children on the way to school and you think how crisp and loving and well-adjusted they all look. Even the man walking the small black terrier is shimmering in a kind of idealistic haze: he says something to the dog, as the dog raises its leg against the lamppost, and you think, *Wow! That dog understands Swedish!* You are stirred up with an abashed yet fervent longing; you have a confused sense that the city is looking back at you from the stage, returning your gaze, singing especially to you.

Yet there was something for me about Stockholm that went beyond all the usual travel-induced fantasies about what it might be like to be from and of a place. From the moment we had arrived and started walking, I had felt both comfortable and intoxicated. A whiff of the Northern Europe I'd grown up with, from my German father and grandmother. This city, even though it was not their city, had the same mix of things I'd sensed in both of them, the dark stuffy villas and complacent mercantile buildings but also a feeling of lightness, of having escaped from that rigid conformity into something fleet and modern. A wry stoicism. A kind of self-deprecating chivalry, a quiet sense of order. White candles burning. Dark bread and herring. "These are the new little potatoes of spring. We just got them," the waiter said, as he put our plates down in front of us. My husband and I were having lunch in an old restaurant we'd come upon, whose name I recognized. "My father told me about this place once, he liked it, let's go in," I'd said. Only when we were inside, sitting at a table, had I realized that my father could not possibly have recommended this place to me because he had never, as far as I knew, been to Stockholm. But I'd been right that it was exactly the kind of restaurant he had liked – old wood paneling, heavy white damask, excellent simple food. The expert waiter, otherwise silent, making an exception to his own professional taciturnity to mention quietly, with genuine happiness and certainty that this happiness would be shared by his customer, the new spring potatoes: this was exactly the kind of thing my father would have appreciated.

"Would have," I say. I ascribe all kinds of reactions, thoughts, and feelings to him, and to my mother too. The longer they have been dead the more I do this, reassembling the pieces of what I knew of them – what I thought they felt and wished for and imagined and feared, what disappointed them or defeated them or made them angry – into shapes that seem to belong to me more than they can belong, now, to themselves.

At the time of this first Stockholm trip, my mother had been dead for almost five years, my father for more than twenty. I was fifty-six. Not only was time passing, time's passing was happening to me.

It was on the last morning of our trip – the trip that, as far as I knew, would be our only visit to Stockholm; if someone had told me then that I could become obsessed with a seventeenth-century failed warship I wouldn't have believed it – that my husband and I went to see the *Vasa*.

We got to the museum before it opened and there was already a long line, wrapping almost all the way around the building. We settled in to wait. The sun was hot. In front of us a Finnish family ate ice cream cones, the melting ice cream dripping along their forearms. Behind us two American couples complained about how long this was taking, how slowly the line was moving. "Do we really want to wait around for this?" they said. "Let's just go."

The line crept along. Slowly we worked our way around to the entrance side of the building. "This is ridiculous," one of the men behind us said. "Look, there's no line at the door that says GROUPS. You see that? Why don't they start letting people in through that door?"

He broke away from the line and started heading toward the door marked GROUPS.

"Tony!" one of the women called after him.

"What," he said, "*we're* a group, right? Come on."

"Tony!"

He was at the door, gesturing for them to come, they were laughing and protesting but eventually they went, and whoever was stationed at that door let them in.

I rolled my eyes at my husband – can you believe the rudeness? – disapproving but also a little envious. Shifting from foot to foot. Not wanting to cut the line, but wishing we could get inside, already: wanting to speed things up, to see the ship and then leave.

I.

THE RECKONING

FIRST SIGHT OF THE SHIP IN THE MUSEUM

Polished waxen ghost of a ship,
but you are the ship.
How can an absence
fill up all this space?

THE SHIPBUILDER'S WIDOW

You had his death and then some months
before you understood what he had left you:
That fucking ship. I can't presume to know your voice,
but that one is my mother's.
She would have understood that part:
The ship that was supposed to be so great,
such glory, sunk. The thing your husband built
to make his name, to keep you safe,
the things he promised you could count on –
him, the ship, his reputation –
gone. And you still here, no longer a wife,
or widow of a master shipbuilder,
but something new: A woman people point at,
pity, blame. A culprit. Married to disgrace.
Surviving and wrecked. Your life changed in an hour.
"Can you imagine?" my mother would have said.

I imagine her saying it to my father,
years ago, before she knew their ending.
If they had gone to Sweden
they might have stood before the dim carved diorama:
You in your nunlike widow's weeds, greeting the king
who came to see you and the ship when it was finished.
That valiant moment: You ennobled, having carried on
after losing your husband, not knowing all you still could lose.
My father loved boats. My mother loved a drama.
She would have asked him if he could imagine.
He would have been silent. Maybe he couldn't.

4

Or maybe he could, and that was why he didn't want to.

But here's the thing. That "Can you imagine?" –
the question she would have asked in the museum
on that imaginary visit long before my father killed himself
and left her with the wreckage of his life, his business –
she kept asking. All her life, before his death and after,
she looked at other people's lives and their disasters,
cheating husbands, drowning kids, sober friends
who started calling late at night and slurred their words.
She'd call and ask me if I could imagine. She wanted an answer.
Yes? No? Could I? Couldn't she, by now?
Those moments when it goes from being this kind of life
to that kind: Don't we all have them?

"That fucking ship," she would have said, if she'd been you,
or if she and I had ever had a chance to go to Sweden
before she got sick, before she couldn't walk, couldn't see,
before she ended up in one of those places
she had made me swear I'd never let her go to,
and I had sworn and meant it.
If she and I had ever gone to Sweden
we might have stood together before that diorama,
your carved likeness, which probably is nothing like you
carved by someone who never saw you
and only thought to freeze you in that ceremony:
The visit from the king, the ship in the cradle,
the dignity with which you tried to finish
what your husband started, without yet knowing what it was.

THE RECKONING

No one knows quite what it was, or how it went:
it happened in secret, among the shipwrights,
who reckoned, and judged her fine. She wasn't.
She was wrong from the beginning – top-heavy,
or badly ballasted, or with a greedy extra row of gunports
too close to the waterline. She was doomed, they all agreed
at the inquest, right after it happened. And still, today,
they are not sure. It was this, and it was this,
or it was this, I have said about my father and the gun,
reckoning – maybe just as he did, maybe not –
the way things could have gone, the way they had to go.

SURFACING

Where do you go, what do you do,
when the thing that couldn't happen happens?
When it's ten minutes in, and you're not under sail,
you're under water. Well, you surface: that's first.
You don't think yet of the luck, to have been
where you were and not at some other post
that would have pinioned and put you down
among the men who are at this moment
becoming members of the crew they'll belong to
from now on: The lost. You surface.
Up here the water boils with screams
and the sudden crazed sound of your breathing.
You swim. Thank God you can. Some can't.
You pass them without thinking, though later, and from then on,
you will think of them, and of everything else
you couldn't help. What's it like,
this thoughtless swim? pulling yourself
through the heavy water, stroke by stroke
toward shore. You're separating from that other story –
storms, boredom, warfare – that thing
we call the future before we know
it isn't. You swim. You haul yourself out
of the water, sit on the shore and cough
with a lot of other coughing guys.
The sun is hot. Whatever clothing
you are wearing – the stuff you didn't
shed in the water – dries. At some point
you get up and walk barefoot back

to wherever you had been staying:
home, or a billet, or barracks. What else
is there to do? You eat a meal
you hadn't planned to eat, a loaf
of bread that someone baked
for anyone but you.

THE GUST OF WIND

It's not like you were a sniper, crouching in a window
waiting for a motorcade; or a loan shark's henchman,
businesslike but brutal, bent on demonstrating consequence;
or someone driving drunk. You came down through the cliffs
that afternoon, through a gap in the cliffs. Hell, most ships
would have loved you. The sails would have swelled and bellied
at your touch, the hull would have rocked and heeled and moved –
you would have moved that thing. You never meant
to kill anyone. You didn't even realize, right away.
You looked back over your shoulder, kind of proudly
(the dash with which you'd gone through!),
and that's when you saw what you had done.
You couldn't get away fast enough.
No one saw you, blamed you, even thought about you,
then or at the inquest. You were nothing, compared to what
that ship would have met at sea. Was this
supposed to be a comfort: the culprit
wasn't your strength, but the ship's weakness?
If there was a tavern where the winds went to drink,
you would have gone there. The other gusts of other winds,
in after a long day or night, would have murmured
and blustered things to you – *Hey man, you were only*
doing your job. We blow, that's what we do; and
That ship was crank, man, seriously. It was her, not you –
but you would have heard their secret relief that it was you,
not they, who sat there spooked and shaking. God knows,
they might have done more damage on that day than you did,
might be coming in from storms, typhoons, tornadoes.

9

All over the world, they'd been lifting houses,
toppling trees, helping fires run through paper-dry forests,
beating at ships until the ships were forced to crush themselves
against the rocks. But this was all on purpose:
unfortunate (or maybe not – some of those gusts of wind
were sadists, bullies, loved this stuff), but part of the job.
It had to be done. Collateral damage. But you –
you were only playing, tumbling along in the afternoon sun
between those cliffs, humming, composing a tune.
A little something of your own, you thought, though
even now you aren't sure exactly what you are
or what it is you do, or whom, if anyone, you report to;
or whether, now, you're done or simply waiting.
The job description: no one has it. Would it matter?
Is what you are a gust? A thing that's separate from,
and subject to, the wind – its product? A scribe
who takes dictation, a follower of orders?
Or are you, yourself, the wind, the one whose judged
or misjudged gusting made that ship go down?

GRAPPLING

Anders Franzén – 25 August 1956

Every day for three summers –
(but already I'm romancing,

swelling fact into legend.
It couldn't have been every day.

There must have been storms,
and mornings when you couldn't

wheedle a boat, or had engine trouble,
or a friend's wedding you had to go to,

or a cold with fever)
– many days, then, you crossed the harbor,

searching for what you knew
(well, were pretty sure – hoped –

often doubted) was there.
You were the fool in the motorboat,

the guy with the grappling hook.
Oh, him. The treasure-seeker.

The scholar. The obsessive.
That sucker for a good myth.

The world's worst fisherman.
The crap you caught!

Old bedsteads. Tires. Stoves.
The bones of a Christmas tree.

You'd list these items later,
every time you told the story,

but sometimes you added
ladies' bicycles, dead cats.

The happy, shuddery wrongness
of all those wrong old girlfriends.

Funny now, but nothing to laugh at then,
when you were gripped by longing.

Couldn't find what you wanted
and couldn't stop looking,

couldn't know your own story
or the ship's – whether failure served

as prelude to a later triumph,
or just as failure.

Each of you lost without the other.
No one to remember. Nothing to tell.

On my desk there is a dictionary.
2. The act of grappling.

*3. A contest in which the participants
attempt to clutch or grip each other.*

Again, I am wrestling with romance,
how to write this,

and what I'd like to ask you.
One day the grapple caught on something.

The probe brought something up.
A plug of oak. Black oak.

That moment when you called
and got an answer,

prosaic and inaudible to anyone but you,
you knew her voice and what she meant.

The story swung into view,
and you and she were its first readers.

All those years you dragged the harbor,
did you think that she was searching too?

THE FIRST DIVE

Per Edvin Fälting – 4 September 1956

Jump. Sink. Keep sinking. Hit bottom.
Grope. Feel nothing. Grope. Grope.
The only sound's your breathing
– don't listen – and the only sight
is darkness. Grope. And here it is,
that thing you call "the object."
This is your official charge today:
a large object, lying under
a hundred feet of water,
has been discovered. Investigate.
Know what you have found
and make yourself not know.
Call each thing what it is,
and only what it is. A wall.
An opening, small and square.
Then, to the left, more wall,
and then another opening, square.
Only after working down
the wall's full curved planked length
are you willing to call these sequenced interruptions
a row of gunports. "A row of gunports"
equals "Ship." Grope. Two rows
can mean only one thing, one ship.
This one. Forget about the darkness.
The thing that was the flaw in her design
is how you know her, and why she's here.

NATIONAL GEOGRAPHIC, JANUARY 1962

You still remember the blue of it,
that issue and its oceans.
The junks of Hong Kong harbor.
The lemon shark, its frantic, deadly eye;
the divers with their fins and bubbles
somewhere off Key Largo. Off Peru at night,
the men of Easter Island lured fish with torches
and traded everything for cigarettes. Here, the story told you,
dreams foreshadowed the future. You were six, and a reader.
You told me once you didn't remember anything.
Another time you said you could remember
sitting under the table in the dining room
trying not to hear them fighting, and the sound
of your mother crying. I imagine you down there,
reading and re-reading the story of *Vasa,*
memorizing every picture, puzzling over the order –
the heeling ship, the sinking ship, the risen ship,
the sunken ship, the battered risen ship again –
clinging to the table leg, pretending it was a mast.

II.

THE EXHIBITS

THE EXHIBITS

The accident was not just the wreck, but the juxtapositions
that should have been fleeting:
this game-board, that cooking pot,
these particular scraps of leather,
that gold ring.

My family, any family:
two people who met on a train,
their parents having met in a reading group,
or a dance class in Berlin.

These bones, in a separate case now,
but lying next to,
having been untangled from, those.

THE OWNER OF THE SKULL

I mean you. Not the museum
or the Swedish government, but you,
the man who lived in it, in whom it lived.
Whatever stories you had heard of shipwrecks
you didn't hear this one. You knew
in the violent suck and torrent
that this was final. Maybe you thought of heaven,
Christ, whatever you'd been taught.
You never thought of a diver.

You never thought they'd build another man
using your scaffolding. They've given him
a face, and hair, some freckles, moles.
You wouldn't know yourself. His name, they say,
is "Filip" – the quotes marking the place
where knowledge leaves off and fiction begins.
No one knows your name. More people see him
in a day than saw you in your lifetime.
He lives in your bones, lays claim to your possessions,
your clothes, your knife sheath, and your coins –
four of them. He's taken everything you had.
He, they say, still had two milk teeth, hidden behind
permanent teeth in his lower jaw. Those tiny
pointed secrets that only your tongue knew
and never could have told because they
were so much a part of you that you
never knew you had them. *He had two milk teeth,*
the label says, meaning Filip, meaning you.

The book on my desk is open to the pictures
of your skull and Filip, the wrong blue eyes
staring from your sockets. Maybe being found, restored,
is just a different way of being lost. Come back,
I want to say, to my father and my mother.
Be who you were, and not who I try to make of you.

THE SHOES

In one man's locker, two pairs of shoes.
In case one pair got wet?

If irony could sink ships
we would all go straight to the bottom.

THE GAME BOARD

Everyone who sees it thinks the same thing:
Oh, I know how to play that game. More, even, than the skulls
that board with its sturdy wooden pieces is something
we recognize as ours. We could have sat there playing
in a tavern, say, before the *Vasa* sailed,
and would not have imagined that this thing, about to be lost,
could have an afterlife.

A Harvard mathematician says the game of backgammon
is finite. Every roll of the dice increases
the probability of an ending, though you could follow the "9"s
that follow the decimal point forever. But how can
an infinite number of chances prove that chance is finite?
Even though we can never get to the end,
there is an end? A theologian would say the opposite:
that eternity is no less real for being unimaginable.

The board is lying open in the case.
The water erased whatever marks were on the dice,
but the game's still waiting for the players
to take their turns. So where does that leave us,
when the last breath is only the last
because the next one fails to follow it?

AN ERODED LION

Not just your face, but your confidence.
Everything you knew about how things worked.
The ones that fell off and buried themselves in mud
retained a shape and clarity of feature,
while you hung on and lost it all.
All the way through this, the things that succeeded failed,
and the things that failed succeeded.

The water had its way with you. Currents
elided your points and angles, rotted your teeth
and the curls of your mane. Bacteria and sulphur
ate you from inside, erasing your tongue.
All that remains is your structure, your outline,
an implication of what you were.
Your face is blurred as if you still were down there
with fish still swilling your astonished gaze.

They've made a separate case for you.
There are two kinds of lion and you're the lesser.
Your adjective defines you. Your label – *An eroded lion* –
cautionary: look what might have happened to the others
but didn't. You face the ship, with all its lions,
Nemean; dynastic; Christian; and the looming roaring
figurehead, brought out of the sea in sections –
the tail, and then the head and body – restored
and rushing forward, resuming the fearless lunge begun
and interrupted centuries ago. The ones you looked like,

the gun-port lion masks, hang on the ship in polished rows,
awaiting further orders. They stare at you like museum-goers,
condescending to the bones.

DEVIL WITH THE WINGS OF AN ANGEL
(WIDTH 10 INCHES)

You were carved, the booklet says,
to announce the royal power,
to maintain the morale of the crew, and
to frighten the enemy.
Let's avoid the obvious comment here,
and say only that you are very small
and would have been all but invisible
at sea.

You were part of a multitude,
an array, a choir of might
that never sang together,
but broke apart. You broke away
and fell. And here you are, back from the depths
with a label. This is what you were made for:
to hang there jeering
at your maker.

THE BRONZE CANNON, 1962

You were jetting to Seattle, to open the World's Fair.
The theme was the future and modern technology,
which you had been once. Now you were famous
for being ancient, part of *Vasa*'s sensational resurrection.
You must have gone in a crate, but
I imagine you strapped into a seat,
looking out the window as you flew
west over the Atlantic, the stewardesses
making sure you had everything you wanted,
and taking you up to meet the pilot,
as they did with dignitaries in those days.

April. The fair opening: a PR firm's giddy brew.
They stuffed you full of shot and let you
boom out a twenty-one-gun salute. The clock
that had for years been dumbly counting down
the days, hours, minutes, and seconds to the fair
stood at 000:00:00:00. The president called
from Florida and talked about the future,
and pressed a button that brought a signal in
from outer space, an impulse from a star,
a wave of sound that had traveled
ten thousand years to reach the fair.

We were the center. The past and future
converged in us and stood at zero, as if
nothing began and nothing ended and

nothing could not be ours, if we
knew enough and grabbed enough or
waited long enough. You were an object
that shouldn't have been there – but really,
what should have been there? The water-skiers
circling a ring-shaped pool inside the stadium?
The Girls of the Galaxy, dancing naked in a sideshow
while men lined up to photograph them?

And where should you have been? You were
the world's flâneur, at home on land or sea
or undersea, spanning continents and centuries.
You sat for six months in the Sweden pavilion,
amid weavings and folk carvings; little boys
said "wow" and stroked your obsolescent lip and barrel.
Then it was October. The end. You and Tchaikovsky
boomed away to fireworks, Napoleon's defeat,
while ships loaded with Russian missiles
steamed toward Cuba. The president, traveling
to Seattle, faked a cold and turned back.

Work on the Cuban silos was speeding up,
not slowing, in response to U.S. warnings.
Negotiate? Blockade? Bomb? We cannot imagine
the future, and cannot really grasp the past,
its antique terrors. Whatever words
he would have said to close the fair were lost,
and no one got to hear the message

transmitted back to earth by a space probe
as it flew past Venus to begin an orbit of the sun –
a loop that, it was said, would last forever,
surviving even us.

COW BONE, SHEEP BONE,
PIG BONE, FISH BONE

I wish I could open the glass case
where you lie in a little row
and carry you down two flights
to show you the bones of the men
who would have picked you clean.

THE TWENTY-ONE CARDBOARD BOXES
FILLED WITH HERRING BONES

Whose crazy project was this? Who sifted and sorted
these miniscule wisps of bone – each no bigger
than an eyelash – into separate cardboard boxes
according to type: one for jaws, another
for dorsal fins, another for spines and ribs?
The cook in *Vasa*'s galley never had a chance
to scoop the herring from the barrel – never
saw the fish, never saw anything beyond
the number of barrels, and his own satisfied or disgruntled
calculations: scoops times men times predicted length of voyage.
He wouldn't have noticed, either, that one of the bricks
inside the galley's massive virgin hearth
was dimpled with the footprint of an animal. A sheep? A cow?
A pig, will be the conclusion of the zoologist who will one day
examine the brick in the museum. Nothing that was found
went unaccounted for. Not a sparrow falls
without God doing something, though what it is
depends on the translation. In some he knows,
in some he cares, in some he gives permission.
So: are we seen, or watched over? Is everything foreordained?
Some herring were sent back to sea in a barrel and submerged
in the hold of a sunken ship for three hundred years.
A pig once walked through a brickyard before the clay
had dried. This is as much as it is possible to know.

THE SMALLEST OF *VASA*'S SAILS

Your tense is the conditional. You would
have been hoisted, if the ship had made it
out of the harbor. In a good wind you would
have been useful. Not in any showy way – you wouldn't
have been the tuba in the marching band,
or one of the drums. You might
have been a piccolo: helping with tone and balance,
moving along with the troupe. You wouldn't
have been good in an emergency. "If
this had been an actual emergency," they say on TV,
after that frantic shrieking beep when they're testing the system,
"the sound you just heard would
have been followed by further instructions." On 9/11
when I watched TV all morning, there were no beeps
or further instructions. I remember thinking,
So what do they mean by an actual emergency?
before I walked to the hospital with my husband
but they didn't want our blood, and then to school
where other parents also showed up early.
We stood there under the sky and waited for our children.
You rode out the disaster folded in a locker,
and that's where they found you when they raised the ship again.
Three hundred years with nothing to do but wonder if
there was anything else you could
have done. You hang in the case, your tatters
spread on a dark background. Your flax threads

glitter like gold filaments. It took them years
to gently piece together all they could,
though you are still in shreds, like a passing cloud.

TORE

I am too superstitious to write this one,
and if you are a parent, I don't need to.
I will just tell you what it says on the label –
"Tore, a tall teenager" – and what there is in the case,
all there is in the case:
the top two-thirds of a skull,
the bones of a left arm and shoulder,
one side of a pelvis.

THE KEY

You couldn't have left it on, or next to,
whatever it opened. The point of a key
is to go away from its lock, to be someplace else,
distant or hidden: to unlock something
but also, by being absent, to keep it locked. A desk, a box,
a drawer, a condominium in Bethel, Connecticut –
who knows what my mother's keys were for,
those keys I still hang on to. When you died
in *Vasa*'s wreck with the key in your pocket,
how long did it take them, on shore,
to force open whatever locked and keyless
thing you'd left? This is not a question
that occurs to the key – now, in the museum,
or during all those years when it lay in your rotting pocket
in the mud beneath the harbor. As far as it knows,
the lock's still locked on shore,
and everything depends on their reunion.

ETERNITY

It isn't possible to see them all at once –
no vantage point is high enough –
but three films are always looping
endlessly, separately, each in its own
dark corner of the museum:
The man who lifts the ax above his head
and brings it down, chopping
at some invisible enemy, swinging and swinging,
never resting and never hitting anything;
the osteologist, with her little dentist tool,
holding a skull, picking at the teeth,
examining, analyzing, forming conclusions
both right and mistaken, picking relentlessly,
picking and picking;
and the voices from the inquest,
which never stop asking "So whose fault was it?"
and "What did you do wrong?"

THE PELICAN BUTTON

No one would have looked closely enough
to decipher this tiny story-in-relief:
the pelican pecking its breast and drawing blood
to feed its young. A Christian allegory.
At least that's what the label says.
Who made this cryptic silver thing?
What garment was it meant
to hold together? A thing this small
is a secret. Even in the lighted case
I can't make out the shapes. I have to take
on faith that what I'm told is here
is here: that the bird's self-murder is an act
of mercy, that the young would want this blood
and drink it, that every wreck saves someone.

III.

THE DRY DOCK

THE PROBLEM

Such a theatrical loneliness,
that could be could be undone at any moment
by a phone call or a plane ride.
Did I come here to find it, or create it?

It's almost winter. I could have told you
before I got here what I would see:
the big skies full of hurrying, uneasy daylight;
the yellow beech leaves shocked and whirling;
the *Vasa* bones; and the room of little Strindberg seas
,in the Nordiska Museum.
Who or what am I missing?

Now you're making yourself cry,
my mother used to say when I was a child
which, as she meant it to, would usually stop it.

What's the problem? she would say
if she were here.

THE KATARINA CHURCHYARD

This morning in the park behind the Katarina church
there was a bride. This afternoon – it's four, and getting dark –
there is a candle, and another, burning in the grass
among the graves. All Hallows' Eve.

Tonight the city has another layer. The elevator
will take us to a lower floor, one that's always there,
but almost always locked. She wouldn't care,
I thought after my mother died,

when they asked what clothes we wanted them
to dress her in. My sister said it mattered,
and chose a dress for them to burn. My mother
would have rolled her eyes. *Dead is dead,*

she would have said, and I agreed, not knowing that
this honoring-the-dead thing that would have felt to her,
and felt to me, then, like evasion,
would come to seem its opposite, by candlelight

in Stockholm, after seven years. *Morbid,* she said,
that summer in the Rhineland when I was nine
and the great-aunt died while sitting up in bed and giving
    orders to the cook,
and the grandchildren were sent upstairs to kiss the body

and then came down to play. The lunch was tongue.
The uncle cried. I remember the sound of it –
loud gulping sobs – and the taste buds,
which made it look like what it was.

THE MAN IN THE WHEELCHAIR

They are hauling him out of a van in the parking lot of the Stockholm Maritime Museum, where I have come in search of other wrecks. Those clanking chains: I'd forgotten them. The shock of seeing my mother in her wheelchair chained in the van that was taking us from hospital to doctor's office, or the other way around. Their iron slap and judder against the metal floor at every bump and corner, their hypnotic awful heavy slither and the way we never mentioned them.

This museum is light and sparse. Long bright halls full of air. Eras of the Swedish navy. Commercial shipping. Pirates and corsairs. The fate of an eighteenth-century pleasure yacht.

And "Sex and the Sea" – dark, open suitcases full of penis photographs, women's underwear, postcards and letters. Double coconuts, convexities, concavities. Soaps and prophylactics, photos and charts identifying many different kinds of sores. The helplessness of men, and women too, the pent-up weeks of waves and empty sky, the darkness of the port.

Behind the curtains, in an inner room, the movie never starts or stops, just keeps looping. An obese naked woman in a bathing cap, miming the backstroke. Men swimming, filmed from below, their penises floating. Three women, naked, kissing, stroking, licking.

The man in the wheelchair is here, slumped and watching. His attendant sits on a bench nearby, looking at her phone. We are the only people in the room. The film keeps looping through its catalogue of strange desires until nothing's strange.

Did he ask her to bring him? Did they enter this room by chance, and then he told her to stop? Which of them orders the other around, and who is she, and who gets to say what "finished" means?

My mother, in the nursing home, lay in bed until they came to move her to the wheelchair, and sat in the chair until they came to move her to the bed. The next thing would be no more than an undoing of the last thing. The aides would circle and murmur, count aloud to each other – *One Two Three,* heaving her into the lift where she hung, swinging in space, between bed and wheelchair.

She told me she thought about Paris – what it was like to arrive there early in the morning, the light, the taxi, the men in overalls sweeping the streets with twig brooms.

Everything is something someone can't not want.

BOARDING THE SHIP

For years I have wanted this. But she is oddly absent.
Acquiesces, gives me nothing. *Don't look in my pocketbook,*
my mother would say. *Stay out of my dresser.* I wanted,
I wanted, not her lipstick or coins or cigarettes,
but access, all of her, nothing off limits.

After she died I marveled at her neatness. Stamps
and pencils. Jewelry. Papers in labeled folders.
I could go anywhere, look at everything. The drawer
where she kept her brushes and curlers – when I lifted them
I found some strands of hair, soft and dustlike.

Yet even here, clutched and vised and expertly pickled
inside the museum, the ship maintains a purpose,
a fierce, immobile direction. To be still; to be dark;
to let herself be measured, studied, written about; to elude.

BEHIND THE MUSEUM

*Professor Anders Franzén *23.7.1918 †8.12.1993*

Somewhere I saw a picture of the ship after they'd raised her
and preserved her with chemicals and wrapped her in pine
and floated her over to her half-built museum,
before they sealed her in. It's quiet here, and green,
behind the museum, in the little graveyard.
You're in the middle of a section, in the middle of a row,
a citizen among citizens. No family here.
A plain, rough, upright stone: your name and dates.
Embedded in the ground a darker stone remembers you again
and couples your name with *Vasa*'s.
On the Sunday afternoon when I went with my mother
to Sloan Kettering, we sat and waited for her to be admitted,
and talked with histrionic brightness
as if we were in a comedy about someone getting cancer.
Across from us, an old couple – she in a bouclé suit
and he in navy flannel, the clothes they would have worn
to watch a grandchild graduate – sat gripping each other's hands.
A few seats down from them, a man who read a book
rested his feet on either side of his modest canvas duffel.
He was by himself and unperturbed, a seasoned traveler
waiting for the ferry that would take him to the island.

THE DRY DOCK

There's nothing here. What's happened has happened.
The rescued ship was brought here, stayed for a while,
was worked on, then was floated elsewhere.

This is negative space – a vast stone canyon shaped like a ship,
without a ship to fill it. A row of blocks for the hull
to rest on, tires hung high on ropes along the walls,

so that her sides wouldn't scrape against the rock.
All this care and protection and solicitude, this belated gentleness.
Decades before they found the *Vasa,* they blasted out this space

that she would one day fill, dumping the rubble
into the harbor over the wreck, unwittingly burying her deeper.
Can a lost thing become more lost?

To the left, a cave whose murky liquid floor is full of fish,
small, pale and frantic. They can't find their way out
and don't know where they are – what is land and what is water,

and where the seabed is. Above, beyond the concrete wall,
a ship glides by, as if airborne. I think of the hospital
in a city I see now only rarely, from a train,

the big brick building floating on its hill,
the sixth-floor window, second from the end.
Ten years on, and I think my mother still is lying there

behind that window, which is always getting closer
or about to disappear. I am arriving, she is leaving,
the track is curving, the building folds its arms and turns away.

Other ships were here before, and after;
she has no particular claim on this space,
now drained of everything. The depth of it, the chill!

The amount of concrete that it takes
to keep the harbor out – to divide this emptiness
from the force of all that water pressing to get in.

IV.

FURTHERMORE

THE MAN IN THE UPPSALA BOAT GRAVE

1.

I imagine one night you get up
out of your grave in its glass case
and leave your museum.
Your boat's a wreck,
but there's a train nearby.
You ride it down to Stockholm
and find your way to the Vasa Museum,
which is closed but you break in
with a spear or one of the two sea-axes
you were buried with.
You head straight for the bones.
They're a thousand years younger than yours,
but you have a lot to talk about.
How the hell you ended up in these museums.
How your naked bones get looked at,
and your mangled, misinterpreted possessions.
But you don't waste much time on this
or any conversation – you understand each other perfectly,
which is to say you understand
what can't be understood. You might talk a little
about shipbuilding. Or about the mummies
in New York and London, and those things in Pompeii
that look like plaster casts, curling, fleeing –
you might invite them next time. But tonight
is just for neighbors. You loot the café for aquavit,
and the gift shop: chocolate wrapped in pictures

of the *Vasa* under full sail, which she never was.
You board the ship and dance all night.

2.
A year later I take the train to Uppsala again,
and visit your museum again, and see that
what I thought was your grave wasn't.
It's not even a grave, but a drawing of one
spread on the floor under a glass case: the outlines
of everything that was buried with you.
All your weapons and a pot,
a pan, eight bowls, a barrel,
forceps, tweezers, axes, dice,
a feather bed and pillows,
a saddle, halter, five dog leashes, and many animals:
cows, horses, sheep, pigs, some chickens,
but not you. The sign says
    "THE MAN IN THE BOAT GRAVE,"
but there is no outline of a man in the grave.
Under the central pile of drawn weapons
where the drawing of a man should have been,
there is nothing.
He did it, I think. *He really did.*
On the train back to Stockholm,
I'm imagining you, looking out these windows
at these birches, these firs,
these fields of yellow mustard, irrationally bright.
Before we come into the city – rock walls beside the tracks

covered with spray-paint words and letters
that must have meant something to someone, once –
we stop at the airport. Maybe you decided to get off here,
slowing only to put up with another X-ray machine,
knowing they wouldn't find anything.
By now you could be anywhere.

QUESTIONS FOR THE SIX BEAUTY QUEENS ARRIVING IN THE LITTLE ROWBOAT

Who sent you?

Who told you to put on those gowns and come across the water to visit the *Vasa* in June of 1961, six weeks after she was raised?

What had you said that morning to your husband, boy-friend, roommate, mother, younger sister, when you rose from the breakfast table? Did you need help to get the gown on, the heavy velvet skirt, fitted bodice, lace ruff? Did you walk to the boat landing, or did someone give you a ride?

Who kissed you, beat you, lit your cigarettes, thought about you while masturbating, told you you had a future in the movies?

What did you talk about on the way across the harbor? Did you know about the Bay of Pigs, or that the Danish barbers' assistants had been conducting the world's longest strike, but had finally now reached a settlement and returned to work?

Did you like each other? Was there a farm girl, a factory girl, a wild girl, a countess, a scholar, and a sweet maternal one, the way there would have been if this had been a novel about six beauty queens?

What was the contest that had selected and ordered you? The one with the big crown was the winner, clearly, but what about the rest of you? In what order did you rank? Did you mind?

What did you say once you climbed the ladder and stood on the scaffolding erected on or next to the *Vasa*? Who listened? Who cared?

What happened after you climbed back down the ladder, got into the little boat again, and pulled away from the ship? Where did you go from there?

What would you remember, years later, of this day?

Did you keep on being beautiful? For how long? In whose opinion?

FURTHERMORE

In those days you were the ship and she was you.
Labor, setbacks, uncertainty – they did their part
to make it a better story. But you were blessed.
Lions confided in you, nereids swam into your hands.
The sun browned you, the wind played in your hair,
your clothes were old and beside the point –
and that was the point. You wore them without thinking,
and they suited you like daylight. I wonder, though,
about that "furthermore." Maybe it's the translation
from Swedish to English, but I'd have imagined,
from you, a simpler adverb. "Then." Or "also."
Was "furthermore" a crow, a jubilant champagne-spray
of triumph piled on triumph, the hero surveying
his line-up of golden fleeces and monsters' heads,
compliant serpents, friends brought back from Hades?
Everything that could have stopped you, hadn't.
But "furthermore"? A pissed-off, fed-up, cornered word.
Two in the morning, a word you fling at the imaginary pack
that's rushing toward you, or running away
and leaving you behind. "This is dangerous," my father said,

when I stopped the car in the middle of the empty street
the night he told me he had lost his job. *Forced out*,
was how he put it. I was sixteen and learning how to drive.
I stepped on the brake because I couldn't do two things at once:
understand what he had said and check my mirrors, hear him
and signal turns, hear and remember where home was.
He told me to keep going. The car was huge and drove itself –
power steering, power everything. It had come with the job
and would have to be returned. "Are you all right?" I asked,
and he said he was.

You know your story better than anyone,
you knew when it was starting: how possession
leads to dispossession, a job, a ship, a museum, a life.
I want to hold onto everything and know I can't,
but can't stop wanting. The loss will not come
through the door you are guarding, it will steal in
through some other, unwatched, opening. For now
you've had the last word, and you can stand there
on the dock, smiling at the camera, holding that day's salvage:
a wooden mermaid, stunned and staring downward,
beginning to grieve her element.

FOOL

"Lot of 13 back issues
of *The American Scandinavian Review*,
1962 - 1965," ordered from eBay, because
I read in one of my books that sometime
in 1963, this magazine included something
Anders Franzén said about the magician
who tried to locate *Vasa* during the 1920s
using a divining rod made of gold.

PICTURES OF THE DIVE CHIEF

1.

You're rugged, grizzled, wearing a cap, surrounded by four young divers: bare-chested, windblown, taking a break from drilling the tunnels beneath the ship. You all work in darkness, in mud, a hundred feet below the surface of the harbor. No tunnel will collapse on a diver, under the weight of the ship and its thousand tons of stone ballast. In the photo you look like you already know this.

2.

You're in your dive helmet, your face in the small glass circle of the mask reduced to shadows and a nose. You've just surfaced carrying a skull, which you hold as if you haven't got one.

2b.

That isn't fair, or true. Your face behind that mask is somber.

3.

So what is it that makes me want to pick a fight? It's something about your man-of-action face and stance. You're like the boy in Grimm who doesn't know what fear is, who doesn't know what it is to shudder. Here you are, tasting the three-hundred-year-old butter from the wooden keg you brought up from the wreck. You're grinning. "Rancid," you said. A few hours later, your face turned red and blistered. How neat and apt the gods, to have punished you in just that way for rashness.

Maybe I'm jealous that no one told you to stop, or that you didn't listen. Maybe you didn't think of it as hubris, dipping your finger in that butter. Maybe everyone else laughed, too, and I just don't get Swedish humor. Who am I to tell you anything – to imagine anything – about a Swedish warship?

4.
You, the cap, the beautiful young divers again. All of you around a table, drinking coffee, smoking, staring unsmiling at the camera, enduring its interruption. I read somewhere that you were in a coffee ad. Maybe this is it. Drink what he drinks and you'll be like him. Far from offending the gods, you are one.

5.
When a story has two heroes, we choose. Hector or Achilles. Prince Andrey or Pierre. Here you are in a little rowboat, standing next to Franzén, floating just above the *Vasa* on the morning of the last lift when she finally broke the surface. You're about to be the first two men to board her since she sank, and I want only one. I prefer his brains, imagination, romance, the loneliness of having set the story in motion, to your muscle and guts.

5b.

Again I'm being unfair. Franzén had told you, back in
'56, that he was looking for the wreck, but hadn't found
it. You were the one who said the mound on the harbor
bottom deep in the water off Beckholmen was not blasting rubble, as the Navy seemed to think it was.

6.

You in your dive suit and helmet, pulling yourself
over the stern of a small boat. The boat is full of men.
You've just made the first dive, ten days after Franzén's
probe brought up the little plug of oak. You went down
alone, and felt your way around. *No,* you said at first,
your voice floating up to the surface over a telephone
wire, *I'm not seeing anything. It's dark down here. Wait.*
And they waited, and you told them you felt something. Definitely the side of a ship. And then an opening. Square. A row of gunports. And then another row.
They knew – Franzén, and all those other men in the
boat – as soon as they heard this. But you had known
a second before, when you said it. In that second you
were alone with the knowledge and with her.

7.

A drawing. *Vasa,* exactly as she looked when she was
found. The high curve of her stern, the upward thrust
of her one remaining mast, the spindles of her broken
stays. Beneath her, your signature and the date: August
'57. She was still on the seabed, a year after she'd been

found. By then you'd gone down many times. It was always dark. No amount of light could light her. No one could see her, not even you. It's a lover's drawing, delicate, private. You knew her whole, by touch.

3. and 6. reconsidered after seeing 7.
Eating that butter was theater. You eating the butter, me picking fights with you in this piece. We keep proclaiming that whatever we are feeling cannot be awe.

In the picture of you coming out of the water in your dive suit that morning when you first found and touched her, you're looking down, away from the men clustered on the boat. They're waiting for you to tell them everything. Maybe it's just the instant that the camera happened to catch, maybe you are just making sure of your footing on the ladder, but it looks to me as if you're hesitating, staying alone with her for one more moment, before you climb aboard and start to shed your helmet and your airway.

LOVE

Someone I loved told me everyone has one like this –
a helpless, crazy love, the kind that drives you out of character.
I knew when he said this that he was mine, that I wasn't his,
and that this was a mercy. In the museum, you stand
at what would have been the level of the wharf.
The ship looms above you and falls away below,
not launched yet. Or maybe you are standing
on the seabed, and this gloom is the gloom of fathoms
and the hull is sunk in mud, and this thing that you
are wandering toward – don't worry, you'll survive it –
is the wreck.

ORB

archaic : something circular

1.
No ship sets out to be a shipwreck.

2.
On the periphery of this story are two other ships. *Rik-snyckeln* ("Key of the Realm") and *Riksäpplet* ("Orb of the Realm").

3.
It was the accidental rediscovery, in 1920, of *Riksnyck-eln* that first launched the fervor for old warships. The Olschansky Salvage and Diving Company was scaveng-ing the Baltic for sunken naval vessels to sell for scrap metal. A fisherman working nearby caught his net on something underwater, and bribed an Olschansky diver with a bottle of brandy to go down and investigate. The diver found an old shipwreck: "There are cannons down there from the time of Jesus Christ!"

The Olschanskys raised and sold *Riksnyckeln*'s bronze cannons. Then, realizing there was money to be made selling antique black oak timbers to builders, they went searching for other old ships to dynamite.

4.

Next they found *Riksäpplet,* which had gone down in 1676 after a sea-battle. They were blasting the ship apart when a diver was killed; the local doctor signed the death certificate and arranged for the body to be sent back to Stockholm. The Olschansky crew paid the doctor with pieces from the wreck, including a wooden wheel from one of the gun carriages.

5.

The doctor was Franzén's father.

6.

Anders Franzén grew up with that wooden wheel, marveling at its intactness after three centuries underwater. The wrecks his father had seen on a trip to Norway had been riddled with wormholes. But the Baltic – less salty, so not a place where shipworms could thrive – might be littered with other miraculously preserved wrecks.

7.

Might be? Must be.

8.

For years, starting in childhood, he listened to the stories told by fishermen and naval men. He made a map: twelve shipwrecks rumored to be sleeping off the coast of Sweden, built in different shipyards under different kings in different decades (setting off to ruin Poland, setting off to reassure a Polish king with gifts). One of the ships was *Vasa*.

9.

In 1926 the Olschanskys had gone looking for *Vasa*. They'd sent a magician out into the harbor with a divining rod made of gold, who had tried and found nothing. Maybe the divining rod did pick up, but didn't divulge, the presence of the single gold object still on board – a ring. Maybe the ship did not want to be found yet. Maybe gold spoke to gold and agreed to keep silent.

10.

The year before he died, Franzén was interviewed by a young and sympathetic colleague. By this point there were sides to be taken. He was bitter and angry, forced out of the *Vasa* project even though he was the one who'd conceived it and found the ship. He gave up any wish to raise other wrecks. When the young colleague first approached him, asking for help to pinpoint the location of what was left of *Riksnyckeln,* he'd said no.

11.

But then he'd changed his mind and said yes. Couldn't stay away.

12.

Over the years there had been various photos of him in the little boat, holding his homemade core punch. In different coats, in different weathers, young and then older, he went out into the harbor to reenact the moment when he'd found *Vasa*. Binding himself, again and again, to the story.

13.

Which facts belong here? And in what order? To whom does a story belong? No one is solely a hero, or a problem, or a martyr. Nothing fully succeeds or only fails.

14.

The year before he died, Franzén was awarded a professorship. There's a photograph: someone conferring the proper hat on him during a ceremony held at Stockholm City Hall.

15.

To get to that ceremony he must have passed through the doors of City Hall, made of black oak timbers salvaged by the Olschanskys from *Riksäpplet* in the diving operation that yielded the wooden wheel he'd grown up marveling at.

16.

Riksnyckeln, whose accidental rediscovery would start the

shipwreck craze, went down far away from Stockholm, a month after the *Vasa* capsized and only one day after the inquest into the disaster ended, having failed to reach any conclusion.

THE TRAVELS OF THE BONES

Nothing can happen to the dead, how could the dead be harmed when they do not exist?

— Malin Masterton, "Duties to Past Persons"

1.

A femur, brought up from the shipwreck by a diver in 1959. Some ribs. A skull.

2.

More bones – over a thousand – found inside the ship, once it has been raised and brought into the dry dock. Some skeletons entirely, or largely, intact. But other bones dispersed throughout the ship. Perhaps moved by currents, or by earlier attempts at salvage, or by spray from the hoses used to clean tons of mud out of the hull.

3.

An osteologist identifies twelve individuals, giving each one a letter code, from A to L.

4.

The bones of each individual go into a plastic bag. The bags are sealed in a concrete coffin and buried in the naval graveyard in 1963, with full military honors.

5.

Over the next few years, more bones are found by divers probing the mud where the wreck had been lying. Six more individuals, the experts think. These bones are never buried.

6.

In 1989 the grave is opened and the bones are disinterred for further study. Water has seeped into the plastic bags, and the bones, which had suffered very little damage during the three centuries lying at the bottom of the harbor, have now become moldy and fragile. When cleaned, some bones collapse into splinters.

7.

Another osteologist shuffles and reallocates all the bones, based on measurements and appearance. She identifies twenty-five separate individuals. One is only an arm bone, and another is only a tooth. She names them alphabetically, using the male names that constitute the Swedish Armed Forces radio alphabet, from "Adam" to "Zäta." The female skeletons B and Y are designated as "Beata" and "Ylva."

8.

The bones of twelve individuals are put on display in the permanent museum, lying on glittering black aquarium sand in glass cases. The rest of the bones are put into cardboard boxes, each marked with that individual's designated initial, and kept in a storage room beneath the museum.

9.

Starting in 2004, new interest in the bones. Recognition that the earlier analyses were faulty: find-numbers had been lost; bones were not kept together; the second osteologist had been told to ignore the context in which the bones had been found.

10.

Further shufflings and reshufflings, based on limited DNA testing and a re-examination of where the bones had been found. Some of Ivar's bones, erroneously distributed to five other people, are returned to him. Cesar's mandible belongs to David. Two of Kalle's vertebrae belong to Beata; but three of hers are reassigned to Filip. Beata loses two metacarpals to Cesar, but gets a clavicle from Erik, and a tooth back from Niklas which, since the tooth was all there ever was of Niklas, means he never existed. Neither did Martin, Olof, Quintus, or Zäta.

11.

The bones get together and separate again. There's a lot of visiting back and forth between boxes, and some crossing-out in magic marker, like those apartment buildings where the names on the mailboxes are always being written over, and no one can remember who used to live there.

THE PARENTHETICAL MEN
(Martin) (Niklas) (Olof) (Quintus) (Zäta)

One of you was only a tooth, a single molar
which, as it turned out, belonged to someone else.
One of you was no more than an arm bone.
Another was a clavicle, a kneecap,
and part of a finger. You were someone's best guesses
which proved to be wrong. The DNA tests undid
and reallocated whatever had been you
until there was no you. It felt like annihilation.
Still, look how much you got away with.
You were never on the ship, never anywhere at all:
lighter than the lightest of spirits. How free you all were!
Whoever it was that smoked in the bathroom
and set off the fire alarm, it wasn't you.
You broke no one's heart, you never pined,
you never burned with love or shame,
never daydreamed about revenge.
Never blurted anything out, never brooded,
never bombed, never blew it, never betrayed
yourselves or anyone else. Never fell short
of expectations. Never attained what you wanted,
never wanted anything. Your records were exemplary:
no blots, no demerits. No self-pity. Just the facts.
And there were no facts. You imaginary wanderers,
you careless boundless never-weres,
you almost-beings – no matter what happened,
none of it, nothing, was ever your fault.
But there's no eluding those parentheses.

They've got you surrounded, they never relax their grip.
Part of your name is your name's retraction,
turned into an aside, or a whisper, a loss
on a balance sheet, by those two enclosing curves.
In your parenthetical world whatever's being given
is also being taken away. You have always almost
reached the room that you can never reach.

MY FATHER'S SHIPS

On top of my father's dresser in the dark New York apartment, there was a ship. I had to stand on a chair to see it. It was the *Cutty Sark*, my father said. He had put it together before I was born. The ship was big yet miniature, red and black, each porthole articulated and framed, a tiny wooden wheel, taut translucent yellowed sails and the fine knotted threads of the rigging.

Later, when I was six or seven, there was another boat beside it. Named after me: the *Joanie B.* A hull, and two triangular sails, one steeper and smaller than the other. He built it on a card table in the living room, in the evenings when he came home from work. I helped him hold the tools; I watched him pass the threads through eyelets on the deck; together we painted her red and blue. Sometimes on weekends we sailed her in Central Park.

The *Joanie B* is in my basement now, held upright in a vise, dusty and spider-webbed. Her hull is green and yellow – he must have changed the colors after I left home, before he lost his job and was on his way down again, after all those years of climbing up.

He bought a little sailboat with money he inherited after his mother died, and named it *Gryphon*. The wings of an eagle, the body of a lion. He had her painted green and yellow – to match the *Joanie B*, or maybe the *Joanie B* had been painted, all those years ago, to match this boat he dreamed of having in the future.

He had come to America in 1939 on the last ship out of Germany. Here is a photograph of him and his brother and some grim woman in a white uniform who must have been their nurse, standing on the deck of the *SS Bremen*. The ship sailed, I find when I look it up, on August 22, 1939. She was two days away from reaching New York when war was declared and all German ships were ordered to return. The captain kept going, delivering the passengers to New York, snatching my father from jaws he never saw, or never told me about. He never told me that his father was Jewish.

Why do we count a ship's passengers as souls? Or no – we only do that when the ship goes down. With however many souls on board. So-and-so many souls perished. But shouldn't it be the other way around – don't we say, in circumstances other than a shipwreck, that it's the body that perishes, while we hope the soul survives?

A sailing ship in a glass case, on top of a bookshelf in my upstairs hallway. I bought it in an antiques store in Portland, Maine for his sixtieth birthday, a year before he killed himself. I remember buying it, one of those vague, almost panicky purchases. *Here*, I remember thinking, pulling out my checkbook, squinting at this wooden ship – crudely made; crudely painted; but charming, I hoped – *maybe this will appeal to you in some way that I will never understand, maybe it will help you to remember what you love.*

THE ANDERS FRANZÉN PLAYGROUND

Anders Franzén Park had so many safety deficiencies that there was
not enough time to finish inspecting the park in one day.
— Market surveillance of playground equipment,
Swedish Consumer Agency, 2016

Without you there would be no story,
but it isn't yours, you cannot keep hold of it.
Look what time has done to this tiny anarchy –
turned it dark, corroded and splintered
the roofs and ladders, broken all the windows.

It must have been fun once: the little boat,
the diving bell, the collection of shacks and docks
and maps and tools. Nothing finished,
no instructions, everything still to be invented.
Leave them alone, they'll figure it out.

Now everything is dangerous, everything's endangered.
Rusted machinery, hooks and pulleys,
broken posts for tying up ships, sharp-edged
parts of things that once were functional.
The parents are anxious. Over there

is another playground, equally obscure in concept,
but safer: a set of barren dune-like humps – a desert? –
through which a single cautious child slowly
picks her way, going up and down the timid
artificial hills. A year before you died,

you gave an interview, telling the story
yet again, to a younger colleague. You'd been
jostled out of the *Vasa* project, you said,
by "people with sharper elbows." All those books
you'd written thirty years before, the gleam of them,

doused, and turned to bitter injury.
The dispute, unexplained, sits uneasy on the page.
Ten years after my father killed himself,
his business partner wrote and asked to meet with me.
He wanted to tell me his side of things.

I never answered, but not because I thought
I wouldn't believe him. Stairs and ramps,
pieces of boats that end suddenly and go nowhere,
no way to steer them. There are no right angles here.
All of it is leaning, every part is slanted. Nothing is true.

V.

SHIPWORM

UNSEEN

Scanning me for something,
they see the shadow of something else,
which will turn out to be nothing.

I'm on the lookout. Sea and sky
at the horizon, but always the sense
of unseen land that's out there, to be sighted,

doubted, sighted again. It will get clearer,
closer, larger, certain.
A collision is coming

with the finite. My father's gun.
My mother waking up one morning
unable to walk. At what point did they understand –

if ever – the ending of their stories?
I am haunted by a photo of the ship
on the final morning of the lift,

the moment when the thing, so long submerged,
became visible: the water-worn heads
of a pair of wooden knights,

breaking the surface, cautious and astonished.

THE MAN WHO SLEPT ON THE DECK

"Bunks or hammocks were not used. Seamen and soldiers slept on the deck."
– from a display in the Vasa Museum describing life on board

What would have frightened you most upon waking this morning
would have been the stillness – to be on a ship
that is not rolling, or moving up and down,
or moving at all. She's stiller than she would have been
when moored at the quay, but in here there is no quay, no water.
Instead there's this building, finite in every direction.
A ceiling, walls, a floor. Before, there were plans –
arrogant and foolish, maybe, not destined to happen,
but plausible, something at least to look forward to,
or to dread – but now there is nothing. No way forward.
No way back. All these lights, these little exhibits.
You don't need to read the labels
to understand that something terrible has happened.

CAREER OPPORTUNITIES AFTER DEATH

Theatrical prop, skull only (poor Yorick).
High school science teaching aid,
entire skeleton. Must not mind
being joked about, and given crude nicknames,
and being jangled – look, he's dancing –
by teenagers who think they are being original.
Med school cadaver, one-year position.
Museum exhibit, if shipwrecked or mummified.
Artist's prop, skull only, vanitas,
must be willing to pose with burned-out
candle and rotting fruit. Salary
commensurate with experience, no experience
necessary. Fish food. Compost. Ash.

KING DAVID ON THE STERN

For I am a stranger with thee: and a sojourner, as all my fathers were.
O spare me a little, that I may recover my strength: before I go hence,
and be no more seen.
                                                                    —Psalm 39

Your deadly mentor-rival isn't here. Neither is his son,
whom you loved; or the giant whose killing made you a hero;
or the woman you fell for when you watched her bathing;
or the husband you stole her from and sent off to die in a war.
It's just you now, hanging out alone above the rudder
    with your harp,
standing on the head of a monster, begging God to spare you
a little longer. Your songs are written, your sins committed;
and they are always with you. *How much time do I have left?*
You knew all along that this was the question, you know it still.
Everything is hanging, everything's arrested: your crown,
its blurry worn-out opulence; the muscles of your forearm;
your anxious tired sideways glance; the broken strings of
    your harp.
You can't know what's below you, but you have a sense
that even in this stillness there is movement: that you are
    sinking,
or that something else is climbing toward you. You know
there's a lion down there somewhere.

FILM OF STOCKHOLM, 1946

This morning when you turned in bed to hold me I thought of our bones: your rib cage, and the wings of your pelvis turning toward me – the iliac bones, Karin calls them in class. The food we cooked for her last night was over-careful, clumsy; but there were candles on the table, in every holder we own: glass and silver, black iron, and brass, and in their light – in any light – her bones were radiant, the jut of the cheek, the Gothic architecture of the backs of her hands.

She showed us movies her father took in 1946 on their family's trip to Sweden, when she was four. *Oh,* we said, *the Stockholm opera house!* and she said, *Is it? I don't know what anything is, I've never been back there.* But she remembers the people: her mother's family. There they were, brief smiles and shadows amid the florid archways of a building.

The city hall, I said.

My grandmother, she said. *My aunt. And there's my mother.*

The tower. The water. A street, a tram, the palace. *It's still the same,* I said.

The film moved to the country, trees and an old house, a table in the garden, the foundry where her mother grew up. *Look at us, we take up the whole road,* her family – a dozen of them, maybe more – fanned out and walking toward the camera. The fourth boy from the left was the cousin she had a crush on, and the small girl next to him was the one she fought with. *I wonder,* she said, *if any of them are still alive,* as we watched the children diving, over and over, lithe and naked, from the rocks.

Without the hint of color now and then (the blush of the house's siding, the faint blue of the tram), one might have seen the film as black and white, as if the past had always been the past, as if the people had only existed in order to vanish.

Last night I dreamed of that tattered, rattling film, that family walking toward me on the road without sound, without words; and then I was with your mother in a house. She was getting ready to go out, and had given away her things, except for one set of clothes and a handbag. She was old and very weak – as she is now; you and I flinch when the phone rings at some weird hour, we think we hear it ringing when it isn't – and she finished dressing and left. I didn't know what I was supposed to do – close up the house? Stay there and wait, in case your mother came back?

I thought I was alone, but then from the darkness deep inside the house came footsteps, toward me, and then a man, young and dressed in white: a sailor, smiling. I smiled too, admiring the jaunty polished fineness of his cheekbones. *I'm just checking the joint,* he said casually before I could ask what he was doing there; and then you reached for me and I woke up and told you the dream.

We lay together both knowing what he'd meant: "casing," not "checking."

We understood that he'd been waiting all along, hidden in the house, looking at everything, deciding what to steal.

THE OTHER JOAN

It's early and today we're the only ones waiting outside the
    museum –
my husband and I, and the woman who asks what time it opens
and tells us she's from San Francisco. *I was here,* she says, *in '65*
with my husband. We came to see the ship. It wasn't in this
    building yet,
and they hadn't really put it back together – it was
just the bones of it, a piece of wood here and a piece there.
There was a lot of stuff inside it, still. 'We've left it
just the way it was,' they said, but I wondered: Did they?
What they tell me and what happened are different things.
They like to have their story. We agree that it's a beautiful day
and that we like Sweden. She's here to board a cruise ship –
Helsinki, Petersburg, Estonia – with her sister. They travel
    together
every year now. *Your name is Joan?* she says. *So's mine.*
We ask her what the ship was like the last time she saw it.
Jerry was curious, she says. *He was an engineer.*
Magnetics. He was one of the guys who invented
instant replay. He was the one who knew about the ship.
She wonders where her sister has gone – wandered
to the other side of the building, probably, and taken the camera.
It's always nice to revisit a place, she says.
There are other people waiting now – school groups
and some men speaking French. My husband sits close to me
on the low stone wall. *When Jerry and I were here before,*
they were spraying the ship with chemicals, to preserve it.

You just walked around it then, in '65, so you got sprayed too,
and so – she says this with a flourish, it was
something they must have said that day – *we were preserved.*

THE PERPETUAL CALENDAR
IN THE GIFT SHOP

You can mark time and keep it moving,
positioning the red magnetic circles

month by month and day by day without end.
The ship is always sailing, with four sails set,

just as she must have looked
in her last unknowing moment.

THE INFRARED CAMERA

A MILLION BRIGHT LIGHTS
Vasa is affected by your body heat,
your breath and your clothing, which
may be wet from rain.
The museum receives a million visitors
annually. The ship hall accommodates
at most 1,500 people at any one time.
A person gives off approximately 75 watts
of heat. The display uses a heat camera to show
how warm you are.

– from a sign in the Vasa Museum

Too warm. I know already. But the camera insists
on looking, and the screen on making me look:
there, that glowing yellow blur
moving warily, helplessly closer,
is me. The parts that are bare – my hands
my calves, the back of my neck – are even hotter:
red.
We are at the bottom. The darkest part of the museum,
where the keel withdraws
into private black-shadowed blackness,
the ship's underside, the hidden part it rests on.

All the times when my heat has been too much.
Loving and scared I might be doing damage.
Loving and told I'm not the only one who loves
my mother and my father, my sister, a man.

The hand held up to stop me.
The camera that sees, the screen that shows,
the sign that spells it out:
The ship, the massive, fragile warship,
is sinking, and when it sinks we will have sunk it.
It cannot bear the breath and heat of all the lovers
who imagine they are in it, on it, drowning in it.

The sign reads like an accusation, but maybe it's just true:
We are here, and the ship is here to be looked at,
and nothing is impervious or harmless.
Look at us all, in our clothes that may be wet with rain.

IN STORAGE

All the old enmities have been forgiven. On a shelf,
in darkness, the lion lies down with the lamb –
or maybe what looks like a lamb is really
just another lion, worn down into something
lamb-like, made vague and gentle by years
of water. Nothing like time to teach you patience.
What choice do you have? The other lion, the big one
on the shelf across the room, hasn't learned this yet.
He used to hang on the rudder. They've taken him down
because the ship is sinking (still! Even here,
in the museum, her timbers shrink a little more
each year) and he was being crushed.
He hates who he hated. He's twisted
to one side, roaring, still fighting his same
old fight. The Thirty Years' War has been over,
now, for centuries. It must have seemed long at the time.

THE LAST ROOM

Here's a board from inside the dive shack, covered with charcoal drawings – a diver giving flowers to a mermaid, a crayfish crawling toward a glass of schnapps. Names of the divers, initials, dates. Here's their bench, and here's the door handle, carved to look like a massive penis. Guy humor. Two flashlights, a couple of helmets. A diver's glove. An empty bottle of Canadian Club, some words in ballpoint written on the label: *"sista dagen,"* the last dive day.

Here are Franzén's evening clothes, in the corner on a hanger, string of medals pinned to the chest. Rusty but alert: the animate hour after death when the soul recedes but seems retrievable, but keeps receding.

Here's his briefcase, cracked and empty, tapping its leather foot. Fill me with papers, find some urgent errand to send me on.

The walls are lined with anchor cable: shelves and shelves of heavy rope that lay during all those underwater years near barrels of tar and iron cannonballs whose chemicals preserved it. These twisted ropes are kept, along with relics of the dive, in a storage room beneath the ship, next to a room of bones. Nothing survives except by accident. The future is an ossuary — everything jumbled, the sharp particularity and separateness of each of us forgotten.

The room is cold. Already, the crucible is cooling, everything that once was molten becoming hardened.

One of the divers came back to the museum at 80. They brought him down here. He pointed to a name in charcoal on the board from the dive shack. "That's me."

He didn't know whether the divers' telephone (the museum doesn't know either, and doesn't know how it got here) is "a typical example," or the thing itself, the one he remembered with a mouthpiece like the mouth of a trumpet, into which Fälting used to speak from the surface to them, the divers, working below in darkness, reminding them, if they panicked, to breathe.

THE WORK OF THE CARVERS

The warriors, the knights, the Old Testament figures —
all were meant to be seen at a distance.
Yet here is every rivet in their armor,
here are their belt buckles and belt loops and buttons,
here are their careful knuckled fingers. The carvers
couldn't have known that human eyes
would ever see their work up close;
this precision, this integrity,
was all for God. The truth was thought
to matter, and it weathered everything,
the wreck and the centuries on the seabed without
the slightest hope of resurrection. See
these grotesque heads, these mermaids, the king
of Sweden as a child. See, too, the way
the wood has worn, these shadowy peasants,
the dim gods and angels, the many figures
clutching things so old and broken
that we can no longer know what they were
or what made the prophets hold onto them so tightly.

SHIPWORM (TEREDO NAVALIS)

Your life is tunnels. You burrow in,
eat your way home, eliminate, fornicate,
all in the same wet den. You're a fraternity boy
who never leaves the house,
eating, drinking, shitting, releasing sperm.
When that gets boring, you turn female,
filling the tunnel inside you with sperm you suck
from the tunnel you live in. Pure orgy.
In the end the place is trashed –
holes in the walls, the floors, the ceiling.
Are you happy now? Don't you just want more?
Or maybe what looks like decadence
is just plain toil. Those frenzied wooden Gomorrahs
are really testaments to your efficiency –
silos full of grain, hives full of honey,
stores and warehouses piled high with manufactured goods.
If holes are your product, then your negatives are positives.
You build by subtraction, add by taking away.
Every emptiness is an achievement.
Your name shows up in every *Vasa* story,
both names: "Shipworm *(Teredo navalis),*"
the Linnaean taxonomic like a graduate degree
trailing your name so that we will take you seriously.
Who wouldn't, after seeing photographs
of what you can do to a waterlogged piece of timber
in sixteen weeks? What would *Vasa* have looked like
after three hundred years of your devoted attention?
You're the cockroach that didn't eat Cincinnati,

the typhoon that swerved before it hit the island.
What kept you away was salt. You need it, love it, crave it.
Without it there's nothing to talk about, nothing to eat,
nothing to drink, nowhere to live. The Baltic's too bland.
Plenty of other shipwrecks in other oceans,
seasoned just the way you like them.
As a child I learned of death and worms together,
some kid on a bicycle who rode to my house
and sang the song about the hearse and the worms
that would play pinochle on my snout.
I'd never heard of pinochle, but I got the idea.
We were meat. We were helpless. My life,
the eternal day-by-dayness of it, was little and would end.
Everything – the sparkles in the driveway,
the taste of the washcloth, the quiver of the soft-boiled egg,
the strange odor of my parents' pillows, my left thumb
with its bulge from sucking – would go.
Everything I'd thought I owned was rented.
My parents' "We'll take care of you"s
were true as far as they went,
but they didn't go all the way.
There was another world my parents hadn't mentioned.
Maybe they didn't know? I was afraid to tell them or to ask.
The kid on the bicycle knew. The song knew.
There were worms and we were helpless.
Always. All of us. No exceptions.
You, shipworm, *Teredo navalis,* less than a tenth of an inch
from end to end, blind and mindless,
relentlessly debauched or relentlessly industrious –

you eat what you want and you didn't eat this ship.
You didn't want meat without salt.
Creation myths need snakes, some devils, a tempter.
A resurrection story turns on a worm,
a master of corruption who miraculously fails to corrupt.
How fitting that you – you connoisseur of,
you maker of, you lover of holes,
you great creator of nothing –
should fill this story with your absence.

ACKNOWLEDGMENTS

I began working on this book in 2013, after visiting the Vasa Museum for the first time. Over the next six years, I made eight more trips to Stockholm, drawn by the ship and immersing myself in the museum and the city.

As it went along, this project that was intensely personal and solitary – an ongoing conversation with a silent impassive museum object – was enriched by the help of a number of people and institutions.

Thanks to the American Scandinavian Foundation and the Harvard University English Department for generous travel grants.

Special thanks to the photographer Adam Davies, whom I first met when we were both teaching at the Fine Arts Work Center in Provincetown. The restraint and emotional power of his monumental, yet microscopically detailed, photographs moved me to ask if he would be interested in creating a visual counterpoint to my Vasa pieces; and we went on to make several Stockholm trips together. During the pandemic we created two online mixed-media shows, exhibited by the Fine Arts Work Center in Provincetown and by Scandinavia House in New York, pairing Adam's images with recordings of some of my poems. For more on Adam and his work: adamdavies.xyz

The Vasa Museum graciously welcomed me and Adam, allowing us access to the collection, and sharing information and expertise. Warm thanks to Lisa Månsson, Jenny Lind, Fred Hocker, Martina Siegrist Larsson, Irene Lindblom, Monika Ask, Kristin Ytterborg, and Ove Olsen.

And to Walter Robinson, editor and friend.

And as always, with love, to Jay.

Some of these pieces first appeared in the following journals:

AGNI
"*National Geographic,* January 1962"
"The reckoning"
"The exhibits"
"The owner of the skull"
"The man in the Uppsala boat grave"
"Shipworm *(Teredo navalis)*"

Boulevard
"The dry dock"
"The key"
"Behind the museum"

Harvard Review
"The shipbuilder's widow"

Kenyon Review
"The other Joan"
"The work of the carvers"
"King David on the stern"
"The infrared camera"

Oxford Poetry
"The Katarina churchyard"

Poetry
"The travels of the bones"